Beautiful Days

On Leave From Iraq

A Collection of Lyrical Poems

By

Andrea J. Kramer

DEDICATION

These Lyrical Poems are dedicated to my late Aunt and dear friend, Else Ehrenstamm Kramer, to her grandson and my second cousin, Paul Samuel Kurzweil, who died while attending Columbia University, on Route 80 in PA on December 3, 1994 at the age of twenty-one, to my Aunt's famous client, the late, Great Ray Charles, to Rob Light and Harold Frogét at CAA for phoning John McBride in Nashville in 2005, and finally and especially to him, for inviting me to mail and fax material of mine, that Else Brailed for Mr. Charles in 1981…which got me writing to another great musician again, twenty-four years later.

ABOUT THE AUTHOR

Andrea Joan Kramer graduated with a Bachelor of Arts Degree from the Broadcast Communication Arts (BCA) Department at San Francisco State University in the early Eighties. She was one of eleven students to win the accredited Four A's Scholarship, and the only applicant to win for Creative Writing that year. AJ Kramer is a copy writer and poet by nature, and hopes each reader will enjoy, understand, and relate to her words.

Table of Contents

<u>2006</u>

2007

2008

1981

"Sunny Makes Me Stray"
by Andrea J. Kramer December, 1981

It was a cold and dreary day
but I was with Sunny anyway
Sunny says I'm guilty still
when I go against my Will

Other men have made their move
Some were clumsy, others smooth
but the man that captures me
is the one they call "Sunny"

When Will married me
and carried me upstairs to his bedroom
It was Sunny, not the groom,
that made me say "I love you"

I know cheating isn't right,
and I won't put up a fight, but
Sunny, please don't do what's right---
make me stray with you tonight,
make me stray with you tonight

"Rastafarian Man"
by Andrea J. Kramer in 1981

I once was sad and used to grieve,
until I met my neighbor, Steve.
With jet black hair, long down his back,
he wore a cap to hide his weave.

He was a Rastafarian Man,
he made his way the best he can.
His braided locks, like Samson, gave him strength,
under his cap he hid their length.

When Steve appeared at my front door,
I asked him in, did not ignore.
He was as nice as he could be,
and lived in my vicinity

He was a Rastafarian Man,
he made his way the best he can.
His braided locks, like Samson, gave him strength,
under his cap he hid their length.

Now, Steve and I are sharing space,
I'm glad I didn't judge his race.
With braided hair and handsome face,
he brings me love with his embrace
(or: he brings me love, much peace and grace)

He was a Rastafarian Man,
he made his way the best he can.
His braided locks, like Samson, gave him strength,
under his cap he hid their length.

2005

"Like a Real Storm"
by Andrea J. Kramer on April 1, 2005

Like a real storm you shimmer and you shake
Put a chill down my spine
Vibrate like a quake
You're no dozen for a dime

Like a real storm you have many different moods
Don't compare to shallow dudes
Put my pretty knees to knockin'
When you start rollin' and a rockin' over me---

Like a real storm you feed the sea
Like a real storm you come over me
Like a real storm you quench my thirst
Like a real storm you're not like the first

Like a real storm you rumble and you roar
Put my feet up from the floor
You take pity over me and you wash me tenderly

Like a real storm you feed the sea
Like a real storm you come over me
Like a real storm you quench my thirst
Like a real storm you're not like the first

"Where You Been"
by Andrea J. Kramer on April 2, 2005,
revised from December, 1981

Honey, where you been?
It's been such a long, long time
Honey, where you been?
There's no reason, there's no rhyme

I've waited here in this old place,
to move on in life, and still save face
but every day is like the last,
you're in my mind, you're in my past

I can't blame you for leavin' me,
for taken work's no mystery
but telephones and planes exist,
so why don't you at least persist

In reaching me and love again,
the bond we shared, remember when
we took our time and savored it,
we were so good, we were a fit

I'm waiting here, a day, a year
I'm waiting here, will you appear
so I can play like I rehearsed
come willingly, and not coerced

Appear to me in broad daylight
appear to me, now in plain sight
appear to me in the moonlight
appear to me some day or night

Honey, where you been---
It's been such a long, long time
Honey, where you been---
There's no reason, there's no rhyme

"N.B.A. Play'a"
by Andrea J. Kramer on April 8, 2005

Be a constant every day
Be a God sent, that's the way
Always show up when it's time
Always show up first in line

Be a constant force of good
Don't debate it in the 'hood
When your Mama cries and screams,
Don't complain with all your schemes

Just do right and walk away
Live to play another day
So you don't wind up a hood
N.B.A. Play'a---so it's understood

Rise above the very best
Rise above all of the rest
Rise above in your own quest
Rise above like you're NO guest

Be a constant force of good
Be a God sent---understood
Be a constant with the grade
Be a constant---have it made

Be a constant another day
Be a God sent, that's the way

Don't just know your so-called place---
Be a God for every race!

"Stay and Repay Me"
by Andrea J. Kramer on April 10, 2005

Stay and repay me for what I've done
Stay and repay me for who I am
Don't leave our doorstep and walk away
Don't turn this marriage into a sham

Our vows were taken a day in spring
I could not have asked for another thing
We had a Wedding, we had a bond
We heard the blessing down by the pond

The sun was shining until this day, today
So now I guess that it's safe to say
You owe me big-time for what I've done
Instead you leave me---go on the run

Now you have robbed me of that sacred time
Is that illegal---is that a crime?

Stay and repay me for what I've done
Stay and repay me, I'm still someone.

"Do You Even Think of Love?"
by Andrea J. Kramer on April 10, 2005

Don't You Ever tell the truth...
Why are you so very ruthless?

Don't you ever speak your mind...
Wish you had a spine, you're not deaf and blind!

So why do you pretend the angels will descend upon me?
All you do is flatter me, make it seem effortlessly
But the truth is that you have a plan...
work for my Dad and take my hand

Do you even think of Love
or just what you can achieve?
What else is up your sleeve
when it comes to you and me?

All you want is revenue and a country house in Maine
You'll pull me along like some ball and chain...
act as if you feel no pain

All you want is revenue
and a yacht and private plane
Even though I must remain...
you have all there is to gain

Don't you Ever tell the truth?
Don't you Ever speak your mind?

My father tells you---
Go For it, I'm dying on the vine

Why don't you pair up with Him
instead of conning you and me
He likes you for a Businessman---
a partner, don't you see?

But I'm the one who'll pay the price
for hooking up with you
You don't love me---just His money...
so that's just what you'll do

"Chicken Soup"
by Andrea J. Kramer on April 21, 2005

At a bar, I met this Jewish man
Turned out we had a one night stand
But before we said our good-byes
He left his shorts as a surprise

The things were tangled in the sheets
They were plaid, extra large BVD's!
I thought he'd call to get them back,
not leave them along with me in the sack

I sat around and waited for a call
He disappeared and dropped the ball
I got so mad, I called 411
Got his address, wanted this done

Unfortunately, when I tried his line---
the voice on the machine, sounded like mine
I didn't care, I was so pissed
So what if I had really missed

I sent those shorts back to his house
I didn't care about the spouse
I even felt like being bitchier
I enclosed my business card and my picture!

The problem was a big misunderstanding
I knew I called 411 and was really gambling
His wife must have opened up his mail,
saw my picture with those briefs,
started to wail, and then turned pale.

I got a call from this poor guy,
he started to stammer and asked me "Why?"
I said I worked at a gym where they were found,
looked him up on Yahoo.com, and checked around…
Isn't your name John David Sinclair??…
I thought I had your underwear…

"Oh well," I said---"can you send them back??"…
I thought he'd had a heart attack!
He said he'd mail the shorts to my address,
until he told his wife this mess.

Now, they are harassing me, all the time---
they have my address and private line!
This must be the most excitement they can share…
'cause the guy who left his shorts,
never did live there.

The End

"Hell Have No Fury"
by Andrea J. Kramer on April 29, 2005

I've been thinkin'
You've been drinkin'
I'm sick of pickin' up after you

This ain't a mix-up
This ain't a fix-up
I think it's time to call it quits---we're through

You're in my house from dusk 'til dawn
All I do is pray that you will soon be gone
Here I am carin' for you like some newborn
Hell have no fury like a woman scorned

I've been thinkin'
You've been drinkin'
You've been ignorin' me from dusk 'til dawn

Not helpin' with the yard work
Not helpin' with the upkeep
Get off your butt and mow the lawn!

You're in my house from dusk 'til dawn
All I do is pray that you will soon be gone
Here I am carin' for you like some newborn
Hell have no fury like a woman scorned

I've been thinkin'
You've been drinkin'
What did I do to deserve your love?

This ain't a mix-up
This ain't a fix-up
This ain't a union from the Lord above

You're in my house from dusk 'til dawn
All I do is pray that you will soon be gone
Here I am carin' for you like some newborn
Hell have no fury like a woman scorned

"Time Means Nothing"
by Andrea J. Kramer on May 1, 2005

My ring is rusty
My dress is musty
Why don't you trust me
and do what's right?

What is time if it means nothing to you
Who am I if I don't know what to do
How can we be each other's best friend
What is time if not beginning and end

All I care about is every hour that we share
All I care about is whether of not you are still there
My days are filled with total faith
that you and I will play it safe---
Then I take a big step back, and look---
you always were an open book

What is time if it means nothing to you
Who am I if you don't know what to do
How can we be each other's best friend
What is time if not beginning and end

You never promised me a time frame,
for our marriage vows
It's true you used to say
"If it's meant to be, then God allows"

21

But time keeps drifting and slipping by,
and all I ever do is cry,
because it means the both of us,
will never give commitment a try

What is time if it means nothing to you
Who am I if you don't know what to do
How can we be each other's best friend
What is time if not beginning and end

"You Can't Un-ring This Bell"
by Andrea J. Kramer on May 2, 2005

Your back stabbing ways have finally
made me kiss and tell
Your phony attempts at praise help make my story,
not so hard to sell
But I valued our friendship as much as I believe
in heaven and hell
So let me tell you, honey that you can't un-ring this bell

Can't un-ring this bell for me
Can't un-ring this bell you see
Because the damage has been done
I hate to ruin all your fun

Your back stabbing ways
have finally made my temper swell
Your insincere praise
helps make my story flow so well

But I just can't wait to tell you,
you're goin' right straight to hell
'Cause honey what's so great
is that you can't un-ring this bell

Can't un-ring this bell for me
Can't un-ring this bell you see
Because the damage has been done
I hate to ruin all your fun

"(Only) Time Will Tell"
by Andrea J. Kramer on May 7, 2005

It seems I wait for you at home for hours
You show up here with wine and flowers
Ready to prove we have this connection,
with all night love and daily affection
It's going all so incredibly well,
I never feel any hint of rejection
Are you ad libbing or kidding me,
when you say let's take our time and see

Only time will tell how you really feel
God, I love you so very much,
for you I would beg, borrow or steal
Only time will tell how much I'd miss your smile
I love your manner and your ways,
your humor and your romantic style

Only time will tell, is what I say to myself
Then I sigh and take your hand,
I know you love me and understand
But don't you see what you do to me
beyond all other opportunities

With me below and you above,
you made me fall so deeply in love
So, only time will tell, is what you say to me...
That's how you can keep some distance,
and still give me intimacy---

"Drunk With Love"
by Andrea J. Kramer on May 8, 2005

I have suspicions...
that you are seein' someone else
I know I'm not crazy,
are you having one of those spells?

Is she cute as a daisy...
in her skimpy little attire?
Is she driving you crazy,
has she turned you into a liar?

You better sober up
'cause you are cooin' like a dove...
Maybe I'm just wrong,
but it's like you are drunk with love

Drunk with love, drunk with love,
walk ten paces, look ahead not above
Drunk with love, drunk with love...
pull on over to the side of the road
and recon with The Man, above

How did you meet her...
where did you two love birds first talk?
Were you sweet to her...
did you spot her, like some hungry hawk?

'Cause maybe I am wrong,
but you are cooin' like a dove
Baby, sober up with her
and with me be drunk, with love

Drunk with love, drunk with love,
walk ten paces, look ahead not above
Drunk with love, drunk with love...
pull on over to the side of the road and recon
with The Man, above

We went to the ocean...
hoping we could patch things up
We got a motel room...
all you did was fill my cup
Staring at all the bikinis on the sand,
no matter the degree
You smile at those other girls,
and barely notice me

Drunk with love, drunk with love, walk ten paces...
look ahead, not above
Drunk with love, drunk with love...
pull on over to the side of the road...
and recon with The Man, above!

"Don't Do Me No Favors"
by Andrea J. Kramer on May 12, 2005

I'm just a country girl
with very simple needs
but one thing I required
from your actions and your deeds

Was a promise and a vow
that you'd be with me for life
that you'd meet me at the altar
and you'd gladly make me your wife

But lately throughout the days and hours
I feel you pulling away
I don't have magical powers
to make you quit and stay

Don't do me no favors
Don't stay out of fear
Don't do me no favors
I don't need you here
If this is outlasting your feelings for me
Then quit your trespassing and don't disagree

Don't do me no favors
Don't step on my heart
Don't do me no favors go, keep us apart
Don't do me no favors, just get out of here
Don't do me no favors, it's over, my dear

"Beautiful Days" (on leave from Iraq)
by Andrea J. Kramer on May 13, 2005

Mama was bakin' a cherry pie
and I looked up at the bright blue sky
and thought baby, what a beautiful day

Dad was cuttin' the lawn in the back
and I realized I still had to pack
and thought baby, I have to go away

If only I didn't have to leave so soon
but I have to be on a bus by noon
and catch a U.S. plane to hot desert terrain

I may not see you again this year
but, Darlin' I ask you to have no fear
because I love you so just say---
what a beautiful day it is when you are here

Now look ahead and not backward, although
I'll be on tactical alert across the desert
plain---don't make me have to explain

Mama will be reading a new cookbook and
Daddy will be telling you to take a good look
and see---I'm defending our country...

Baby, thank God I had these beautiful days
to spend with you---
that's what's always going to get me through
so I need you just to pray---and say
I'll see you again one beautiful day

"My Broken Family"
by Andrea J. Kramer on June 7, 2005

My father left when I was four
I saw him leave through the back door
My mother cried and held me tight
She whispered it would be alright

So when I would grow up
life couldn't interrupt
or take out its toll
on my spirit or my soul

My mother said to me
there is no secrecy
just keep my chin up high
and believe in decency

And then she said to dream
that I could be redeemed
in my songs about my broken family

My broken family is what has molded me
My Dad was not around so I learned adversity
My Camelot fantasy is what inspired me
I went through all twelve grades, and sang on stage
whenever the band played

My broken family is what has molded me
It made my memories true, and my heart sing out to you

My broken family was not some tragedy---
it taught me how to soar---and believe in myself even
more

"One or the Other"
by Andrea J. Kramer on June 9, 2005

When the plane to Vegas was ready to land
all I could think about was winning my hand

The blackjack table is where I have fun
I play all night (long) until I have won

Then I move on over to the poker game,
throw down my money for more of the same

But when the stakes are high
and my mouth gets dry
how can you help me, brother?

I'm there to win so I'll down my gin
and gamble on one or the other.

Don't make me choose or I just might
lose if I don't gamble on one or the other---
only on one or the other

It's like cheating between my girl-friend and wife---
if I get caught, it'll ruin my life
so brother, don't make me choose on one or the other,
not on one or the other.

"Deidre's Song"
by Andrea J. Kramer, written on July 27, 2005

I take my bow up on the stand
The melody is what I am
The moment's here to sing my score
It won't be long before the critics roar

And if I keep your heart with this
Then I know the sound is right
We should never fight and be apart
It ruins all my days and nights

So I'll sing for you and I'll take a stand
And they'll play for you---that big brass band
Everyone will listen and give a hand---applause,
Applause for my handsome man

You are my prayer, you're in my soul
You and the music are my only goals
And I'm only here to impress you---
I chose money and fame to caress you

So don't be ashamed, and I can't be blamed,
'cause I love you and don't think less of you
But it's time to grow and be stronger so
Notoriety won't always obsess you

I'll sing for you and take a stand
Play for me that big brass band
It's the music that has all the power
It has made you the man of the hour

The glory that makes me adore you
Is the one thing that makes me ignore you---
When you say that you are leaving
I refuse to stop believing

The story that makes me adore you
Comes the moment that you return---
and I feel myself falling deeper,
and I know it is your turn

You will stay with me forever
Because you're a very forgiving soul
I promise you that I'll never
Let my performing take its toll

So I'll sing for you and take a stand
Play for me---that big brass band
Everyone will listen and give a hand
Applause, and praise for my special man.

"Rebel Gal"
by Andrea J. Kramer on July 30, 2005

I'm a rebel gal, and you're not my pal---
You represent the law, and I'm not your squaw
So, Sheriff, take me in---do what you will to me
But I like my men, to show bravery

I'm a gun totin' moll---not a paper doll
and I'm comfortable, in my native skin
So, Sheriff, take me in---do what you will to me---
But, I like my men, to show decency

All us women know---how to bait and fish---
gut and clean our catch---fix a real nice dish---
But, there's more to me---than a cook and clean---
if I have to obey---I'll be downright mean

So, Sheriff, take me in---do what you will to me---
But, I like my men, to show sympathy
I'm a gun totin' moll---not a paper doll---
and I'm not afraid of the infantry

"Thunder"
by Andrea J. Kramer on August 21, 2005

Thunder doesn't have to lead to rain
Sometimes riders take a different train
But think twice before some woman again
pours you a drink, and winks and just says when?

If I give up on you that will be it---
I promise, honey, it won't hurt a bit
I'll just be gone one day when you walk in
That tightrope you've been on is wearing thin

So when I tell you that I want you home
That means you won't have time to prowl and roam
Give up your past time of romancing them---
Because you think I can't meet other men

Oh, honey, thunder mustn't lead to rain
You really don't have all that much to gain---
Clouds and lightning always make me scared---
How could I have known, you would have ever dared---

Thunder doesn't have to lead to rain---
Things can happen that you can't explain---
I think about how much we both will own,
if we just love and leave well enough alone.

"No Longer The Boss"
by Andrea J. Kramer on October 14, 2005

I'm packin' a colt .45 and a .38
In my job I'm not lyin' in wait
I've been told it's the law of the land
to preserve and protect when I take a stand

But the badge that I wear each day
Doesn't make it easier when I pray
to defend what I did last night
when I caught my best friend with my wife.

I lost control when I opened the door
all I could see was them on the floor
rapped around like that snake on the tree
the forbidden apple was their destiny

I felt shame and pain and loss---
I no longer am the boss
I have been doubly betrayed
My wife and friend got me in spades

Here I am with a gun in my hand
I aimed and fired at the lamp on the stand
That got their attention and they stopped and cried---
I looked at both of them and just asked "Why"?

They stammered back at me they were in love---
I pulled the trigger as I aimed above
The bullet grazed his head and hit the wall---
down on his knees he didn't look so tall

I felt shame and pain and loss
I no longer am the boss
I have been doubly betrayed
My wife and friend got me in spades

The gun and badge I wear each day---
no longer matters when I'm on display
I just look at the world as cold---
If life's a poker game---I fold.

"The Relationship Way"
by Andrea J. Kramer on October 21, 2005

I didn't always feel alone
I kept busy with my family and my home
I was a rich man's pretty wife
My life was all about his slippers and his pipe

My cup runneth over every day---
I picked up the kids in my new Range Rover
and went to play
Soccer Mom and tennis pro---
I put on the perfect Millennium show

But the chink in my armor got larger and larger,
when I learned what it meant, when the rich man's
account was spent---

Love and fidelity---
what can you do with it?
There's no relationship first aid kit,
when your mate breaks your heart

Love, what can you say to it---
when your partner gives up and quits,
and your life falls apart---
is there ever a fresh start?

Hope, is all there is to grab---
now it's time for life's rehab,
so you can get out of bed---
and put on a happy face, instead

Faith is all wrapped up in God---
no way you can fake that facade---
when you lean on Him to pray---
better mean what you feel and say

Ask Him, for love to find you a better friend,
who this time will stay loyal until the end,
and make this life a fence to mend---
make this wife a chocolate heart to send,
And not play another "let's pretend,"
this is the relationship way.

"Untitled"
by Andrea J. Kramer on November 7, 2005

When I was twenty-one, I finally met someone
who understood my hopes and dreams
He said we were alike---he'd take me on his bike,
we'd ride for hours at top speed
I'd hold onto his waist---
his helmet covering my face
and the big smile he would bring

We'd see the mountain peaks,
tall pines and winding creeks---
we'd had our fill of sun-streaked days

This road can lead to dust
if you don't love and trust
the friend who helped you to be free

But when he only plays, won't work or change his ways,
somebody has to stop and say

We had our innocence
But now that candle's lit
And it will surely melt away

We had our bones to pick
But that's not scandalous
As long as we grow up some day

I wish we could just ride---I'd never leave your side
But that won't stay a novelty

So Darling, hear me out---
let's take a different route
And travel life's stability

This road can lead to dust,
if you don't love and trust
the friend who helped you to be free

"Kindness, Kisses, Love"
by Andrea J. Kramer November 22, 2005

I wasn't always like this, a happily married man
I used to drink and squander and wander the land
I had no feelings for anyone but myself that would last
To women I seemed appealing until they learned my past

I roamed around and gambled, looking for young things
Their hearts were up for grabs to me---
but it didn't mean a thing

Until she came along one day and got up in my face---
she accused me of being selfish and called me a disgrace

I thought she was a smart one---
who would teach me right from wrong
She nursed me through the tough mans' pain,
until my love was strong

She said I was a goner unless I settled down---
I told her that I bought her a ring and wedding gown

Kindness, kisses, love make me your slave
Till the Lord above puts me in my grave
I belong to her, my heart's on my sleeve
Will she let me stay---give me my reprieve

She says I'm cavalier today about her and the boys---
Well, that's alright from here my Dear, I'm only
making noise

If love was based on fame---
then I've been famous with you before
Give me another chance and I'll be famous one time more

Kindness, kisses, love---make me your slave
Till the Lord above puts me in my grave
I belong to her, my heart's on my sleeve---
Will she let me stay and give me my reprieve

Happy Thanksgiving Y'all!

"I'd Rather Die Than Change a Thing"
by Andrea J. Kramer on December 4, 2005

When we made love I was afraid
My compromise was the bed I made
But you whispered in my ear to believe in you
And when I did my dreams came true

You are the best thing in my life
I rather die than change a thing
You took me out of obscurity
You showed me what riches life could bring

My heart is intertwined with yours
Our children's' smiles are a testament
I never question why this is
I only know to acknowledge it

Our souls have been through this before
You never were a stranger to me
Despite the hectic world we adore
I know the answer is family

You are the best thing in my life
I rather die than change a thing
You are my heart that beats to live
You are the air I need to breathe

"Shade of Gray"
by Andrea J. Kramer on December 18 & 20, 2005

When we first met you said
I'd get a diamond in the rough
We dated a year, all smiles no tears
then we were married---you didn't bluff

Sometimes I think you had it planned right down
to the very last detail
So how did this relationship of ours
ever get derailed?

I have my pride
I won't hide what's inside
I'll find a way to make a shade of gray
Not all break-ups can be just black and white
The layers merge like dusk turns into night

I went along just like a song
that has no real beginning or end
I stuck by you, then you withdrew---
I didn't know how to pretend...or even defend

I have my pride
I won't hide what's inside
I'll find a way to make a shade of gray
Not all break-ups can be just black and white
The layers merge like dusk turns into night

·

All of a sudden, you pushed a button
and my love for you and friendship went away
But you were cruel and were mistaken,
if you thought breakin' my heart was child's play

I have my pride
I won't hide what's inside
I'll find a way to make a shade of gray
Not all break-ups can be just black and white
The layers merge like dusk turns into night

"No More Good-Byes From My Blue Sapphire Eyes"
by Andrea J. Kramer December 20, 2005

I can't begin to describe the way I feel alive from you
I breathe in the day with you not far away
from telling me "I do"
Although ten years have passed
it's still just like our honeymoon
So let me save you time when you know
I'll be coming home real soon

No more good-byes from my blue sapphire eyes
It's no surprise-I'm still in love with you
So let me save us time on our farewells
Although a decade's passed---I still hear wedding bells

While on the road, I miss you all the time
The hectic pace---I still have time to pine
I count the days until I'm in your arms
If love is heat---I set off all alarms

No more good-byes from my blue sapphire eyes
It's no surprise---I'm still in love with you
So let me save us time on our farewells
Although a decade's passed---I still hear wedding bells

It may sound quaint---but I am yours for keeps
I have no restraint---you're even in my dreams
My life is great---I wouldn't change a thing
Somehow I need your eyes to look back at me and gleam

No more good-byes from my blue sapphire eyes
It's no surprise---I'm still in love with you
So let me save us time on our farewells
Although a decade's passed---I still hear wedding bells

"Dorothy---Do You Ever Long For Kansas?"
by Andrea J. Kramer Christmas Eve, 2005

Growing up on my father's farm
where our cows were used for dairy
All that I loved was in front of me,
and I'd thank sweet Mother Mary
It's funny where life can go and take us---
born one place then livin' in the next
Raising a family, cookin' breakfast---
it seems like these places are both blessed

Dorothy--- Do you ever long for Kansas?
I do, but I really love it here
Smoky mountains and green ranches
Nashville has been my home for years

Moses moved his people to the Promised Land---
it took them all of forty years to find
Nashville is where I had a helping hand,
and this is where I have finally found mine

Dorothy--- Do you ever long for Kansas?
I do, but I really love it here
Smoky mountains and green ranches
(or: We don't get all that many chances)
Nashville has become my home frontier
(Nashville is a place that I hold dear)

I found The Emerald City
and a man with courage, brains and heart
I had my three girl babies---
Nashville gave me my fresh start
(or: sets us all apart)

Dorothy---Do you ever long for Kansas?
I do, but I really love it here
Smoky mountains and green ranches
Nashville has been my home for years

"Takin' Care Of You Is Right"
by Andrea J. Kramer
on December 28, 2005 (my birthday)

I'm relaxing on my rocker after bakin' Betty Crocker
and now I am writing my song
Well, it took all afternoon
because you make me want to swoon---
takin' care of my man Isn't wrong.

I look out my front porch, holding an imaginary torch---
thinking---waiting for you is fun
'Cause a man worth lovin'
is like bread bakin' in the oven---
it rises to the occasion when done.

You're livin' proof---takin' care of you is right
It's the God's honest truth---I love being your wife
Livin' under one roof---makes the days go by
I'd jump through hoops---just to be by your side

Well, here I am still collecting my thoughts---
I'm on the lam until your laundry's done
It took all day long---now the groceries are bought---
what can I say-I've only just begun

You're livin' proof---takin' care of you is right
It's the God's honest truth---I love being your wife
Livin' under one roof---makes the days go by
I'd jump through hoops---just to be by your side

A good man can be charming to his wife---
all I can do is see---you and me through life
If it's not destiny---it's just doing the math---
I desperately need to be next to you on your path

You're livin' proof---takin' care of you is right
It's the God's honest truth---I love being your wife
Livin' under one roof---makes the days go by
I'd jump through hoops---just to be by your side

2006

"Martina, Martina"
by Andrea J. Kramer on January 6, 2006
(for a male vocalist)

Martina, Martina with a heart like Athena,
brave and strong and true
The face of an angel, soaring wings in your voice---
the fates would have it
you'd have no other choice but to sing for me and you.

Sing and share your gift, without a care and swift---
the magic in your tone leaves no one alone
Children laugh and play around you,
glad that they have found you---
they will always remember you
and praise you when they're grown.

Not all men dare to match your style---
I know you care deeply I see it in your smile
All of us alike, every man, woman and child
are grateful for the beauty that you inspire.

Martina, Martina with a heart like Athena,
brave and strong and true
The face of an angel, soaring wings in your voice---
the fates would have it
you'd have no other choice but to sing for me and you.

Sing and share your gift, without a care and swift---
the magic in your tone leaves no one alone

Children laugh and play around you,
glad that they have found you---
they will always remember you
and praise you when they're grown.

"Martina, Martina"
by Andrea J. Kramer on January 6, 2006
(revision for a female vocalist)

From the time I was a baby my father sang to me.
He whispered that just maybe
the angels would agree
that when I would grow up there'd be the possibility---

He said Martina, my daughter, this is your destiny,
then he would sing---

Martina, Martina with a heart like Athena,
brave and strong and true---
my gift from an angel, soaring wings in your voice---
the Fates would have it
you'd have no other choice, but to sing for me and you.

Sing and share your gift, without a care and swift---
with magic in your tone, leave no one alone
Children can laugh and play around you,
glad that they have found you---
they will always remember you,
and praise you when they're grown.

Not all others will dare to match your style---
you know how deeply I care, you can see it in my smile.
All of us alike, every man, woman and child
are grateful for the beauty that is inspired.

Martina, Martina with a heart like Athena,
brave and strong and true
my gift from an angel, soaring wings in your voice---
the fates would have it
you'd have no other choice, but to sing for me and you---
It is what you're meant to do.

Sing and share your gift, without a care and swift---
with magic in your tone, leave no one alone.
Children can laugh and play around you,
glad that they have found you---
they will always remember you,
and praise you when they're grown.

"To Have Enough Love"
by Andrea J. Kramer on January 17, 2006

My heart needs healing.
My head is reeling.
I'm so alone.

I had the feeling,
you'd hit the ceiling if I came home,
and told you what needed to be said.

Instead, I did the weakest thing,
I left a note.
Your name's not John,
but I started with "Dear..."
and let you know, what you had feared,
that I was done.

I'm scared to death.
I'm out of breath,
like being on the run.

It's hard to tell, if only I fell out of love,
I look above, and see the sun.

Times are tough, and life is rough,
but I'll make it through,
because I'm due to have enough,
to have enough, enough love.

"There's A Need To Bring"
by Andrea J. Kramer on January 18, 2006

There's a need to sing, that I live to bring.
There's a need for Peace that means everything.
History repeats itself so we can get it right.
Some good men and young women
step up and gladly fight.

Take time to see what's real, acknowledge how you feel.
Clear the air and do what's fair and lessen your ordeal.
(or: don't treat this surreal.)
Take a stand, like brothers band and never feel alone.
Be a man, and Uncle Sam will find a way back home.

There's a love to dream, that I live to bring.
There's a need for hope that can help us cope.
Though history repeats itself, and all its do's and don'ts.
Children grow and need to know,
they're protected by their folks.

Take time to see what's real, acknowledge how you feel.
Clear the air and do what's fair
and make this, strong as steel.
Take a stand, as brothers band, and don't feel all alone.
Be a man and Uncle Sam, will find a way back home.

"Lord, Have Mercy"
by Andrea J. Kramer on January 26 & 28, 2006

Lord, have mercy and that's a fact---
can't get those angel's wings off of your back.
That halo above your head is there for good---
robbing me of greed, like Robin Hood.

You tell me to be generous to a fault---
you say my emotions are locked up inside a vault.
You claim, I am holding back what I feel---
you tell me that my jealousy is not real.

But let me say and I'll even pray
that you are my healer, my spiritual wheeler-dealer,
my saving grace, my reason to race home to see your face,
and then embrace you, day after day, after day...

Lord, have mercy, I cannot be a liar---
the thrill you bring, the sheer desire...
The good in me, that you say you can see,
the honesty that you do so admire...

If you were a cowboy or a rancher for hire,
then I'd be a cowgirl who would warm you by the fire!

Just let me say, and I'll even pray
that you are my healer, my spiritual wheeler-dealer,
my saving grace, my reason to race home to see your face,
be in your space, day after day after day, after day---

You chase the demons away,
keep my hair from turning gray,
you make me dance, and rock and sway---
Oh, Lord have mercy, you make me crave you,
my angel man,
you get me to behave you, angel man,
you angel man---Oh, Lord have Mercy!

"Angel Medley"
A Hymn by Andrea J. Kramer on January 31, 2006

She'll grab you by the hand,
just to let you know she's there.
She'll make a better man of you
to show how much she cares.
And in this dangerous land,
she'll make you even more aware---
that an Angel lady has your back,
and comes to you prepared.

You can feel them---
Oh, you can feel them on the ground and in the air.
You can feel them,
Oh, how you can feel them---yes, they're everywhere.

It seems there are a lot of times,
when peoples' faith runs out.
They march around, and hold up signs
and look for things to shout.
They act as though the answers
will appear to them, unfair.
They reason that the cause is God,
and just look up and stare.

You can feel them---
Oh, but you can feel them on the ground and in the air.
You can feel them...
Oh, how you can feel them---yes, they're everywhere.

I've traveled the world, and worked to play---
my instrument is my voice, they say
To stay clear and sunny on cloudy days---I listen for
angels and give God, praise.

You can hear them…
Oh, and you can feel them on the ground and in the air---
You can hear them...
Oh, how you can hear them---yes, they're everywhere.

"Our World"
by Andrea J. Kramer on February 7, 2006

The world is in danger so go back to the manger
Now Arabic strangers bomb our Road Rangers
In two thousand years since Jesus appeared
Suicide dreamers think they're redeemers

All we do is wait for change,
while we're in their killing range
Will we ever win this war---
more for the rich and less for the poor
But I know that this is true---
what we see is not what we do
Is the purpose oil and fuel---
or will the Iraqis ever rule??

American strangers
Republican gangsters
Tanks and Road Rangers
Desert of danger

Oil and money
Wasteland so sunny
Man, this ain't funny
Republicans' running

"When It Comes To You And The Girls"
by Andrea J. Kramer on February 17, 2006

I'm away from home and my telephone
has the ringer turned down on low.
I miss you and the kids but I'm on the road
and I have to prepare for a show.
I'm so glad that you're my mate
and their big, strong Dad--- that I know they're great,
only a little sad, and when it comes to them and you---
this I know is true---

I'm a nail biter, a warrior fighter,
a fairy princess, a runner for distance,
a homemaker, a giver not a taker,
and a lioness with her cubs---
So when you listen to me, and I'm singin' "Country"---
it's for you and my girls with love.

The folks of Nashville turn no one away---
they welcomed our family and asked us to stay.
So honey, we have a place where our kids can play,
and you have the talent to get me to laugh and say---

That I'm a nail biter, a warrior fighter,
a fairy princess, a runner of distance,
a homemaker, a giver not a taker,
and a lioness with her cubs---

So when you're missing me, and I'm singin' "Country"---
know it's for you and our girls with so much love---
yeah, it's for you and our three girls with love!

"Lovin' A Mysterious Man"
by Andrea J. Kramer on December 23, 2005, revised on
February 25, 2006

Well, here I am singin' my song,
when I collected my thoughts it took all day long
just to say the God's honest truth.
I sat down on my glider, swingin' on the front porch---
I can't believe I held a torch
for this man livin' under my roof---
now, I have all the proof---
that his love is gone.

What is worse than a woman's curse
of lovin' a mysterious man?
A good man who does bad things,
being charming whenever he can.
What's as hard as livin' large
and not saving for a rainy day?
Thinkin' everything's o.k.,
while your kids go out to play.

What is worse than a woman's curse
of lovin' a deceitful man?
A good man who does bad things,
being charming whenever he can---
All I can do is hope that I'm not at the end of my rope,
and I'll find the patience to forgive---
the stamina to find a job,
the wherewithal to live---.

Well, here I am singin' my song,
when I collected my thoughts it took all day long
just to say the way I feel---
I wish it weren't so darn real---

But, I have to likewise confess,
that I contributed to this mess
of lovin' a mysterious man.
One, who I can barely stand.
Yet, one I won't demand
leave us alone, and leave our home,
instead of givin' me a helping hand.

"Red Balloon"
by Andrea J. Kramer on March 8, 2006

What can it be that makes me see
the Lord's surprise in a sunrise?
My child's ill but has the will
to dress herself in a disguise.
Her little body is so frail,
but she puts on her shirt and overalls.
She wants to play on the jungle gym---
she doesn't understand she's small
(or: she doesn't understand she'll fall.)

When she gets up in the mornings---
she says she needs her medicine,
and a great big hug.
I'll make her breakfast, and think to myself,
that all she asks for is my love.

Mama's gonna check on you later
Mama's gotta take you to school
Mama's gonna take you to the doctor's,
and buy you a red balloon.

My child's brave and caring---
she understands about her health.
The doctor's threw with sharing---
he keeps his prognosis to himself.

Mama's gonna check on you later
Mama's gotta get you from school
Mama's gonna take you to play in the park,
and buy you a red balloon.

It seems like winter's over,
and spring's around the bend.
My daughter's not much older---
but an Angel will descend.

Mama's gonna check on you later
Mama's gotta share you with God.
Mama doesn't want you to hate her---
if you understand, just nod.

My child's weaker and weaker---
but keeps up a very brave front.
I wish that I could keep her---
from the sun, rising only once.

Mama's gonna check on you later
Mama's gotta share you with God.
Mama doesn't want you to be scared no more---
if you understand, just nod.

"I Want To"
by Andrea J. Kramer on March 18, 2006

When day-to-day life takes its toll,
the deep blue ocean soothes my soul.
Standing by myself on the sand,
I can't give in to your demands.
You won't let go, until you set things right,
that's what you say from sun-up until night---
So when you tell me that I'm wrong,
your gestures towards me aren't strong.

I want to go to the ocean,
and just talk without a fight
I want to feel some emotion,
whether I'm wrong or right
I want to wade through the water,
and take in the salty air---
I want to bathe in the water,
and know how much you care

You say you won't back down on this one,
and that you'll try to make things right.
But I just want to go to the ocean,
and pray that we don't fight.
I want to walk in the moonlight,
and just hold hands and talk---
I want to wash away our problems,
and not have to watch you like a hawk.

I want to go to the ocean,
and just talk without a fight
I want to feel some emotion,
whether I'm wrong or right
I want to wade through the water,
and take in the salty air---
I want to bathe in the water,
and know how much you care

"Shut My Mouth"
by Andrea J. Kramer on April 2, 2006

Well, shut my mouth if you're not from the South,
and you were not raised in Tennessee.
Then come on down, and look around,
if you want to find Celebrity!
Star-spangled youth is the future---
that's the truth, when it comes to the Grand Ole Opry.
Open up and sing, and remember everything
that your Mama raised you to be!

You had your chance---now sing and dance,
'cause you've moved on to a better place---
Ain't no romance--- being in a trance,
every time you see my name and face.
Open up and sing, and remember everything
that your Mama raised you to be---
Remember your roots,
when you're puttin' on your boots,
spurs, cowboy hat and jeans.

(Sing along with me:)

Well, shut my mouth if you ain't from the South,
and you were not raised in Tennessee---
Then come on down, and look around,
if you want to find Celebrity!
Star-spangled youth is the future---
ain't that the truth, according to the Ole Opry---

Open up and sing, and remember everything
that your Mama raised you to be---al' Right!!

"I Won't Spring Clean"
by Andrea J. Kramer on April 23, 2006

I know there's a war goin' on---
I show my support when I fly the American flag
at my front door.
But I listen to the rhetoric and I just can't ignore---
the way we wait and delay and let our strategy lag,
and our troops deplore... we wait and we negotiate
as we let our jets and bombers soar.

So, I say to myself, just wait---
when I see car bombs in Fallujah
and dead bodies in Kuwait.
I tell myself, I understand---
that this was the future when I voted for The Man.
I tell myself, I'm "Country" smart,
and not to be impatient or put the horse before the cart.
I show my support and buy a banner
down at the Wal-Mart...
I pretend that I don't see
that the world's coming apart.

So, I tell myself the plan is clever,
and that we'll put an end
to Al-Qaeda and terrorism forever.
I want to believe this is true.
But I come home and don't know what else to do
and just think, "Never say never".

But if you want to stop all this pain---
then I guess that it's best for the troops there to remain.
I won't ever understand---
why we listen to the lies
and believe that they're first hand.
But, I can tell you that this much is true---
the U. S. of A. will determine what to do.

Hmm, hmm, hmm, hmm, hmm, hmm,
hmm, hmm, hmm, hmm, hmm, hmm---
That the U. S. of A. will determine what to do.

"Short Lived"
by Andrea J. Kramer on June 25, 2006

I won't walk through this door, anymore---so help me
I will no longer play tug of war---can't you see?
I'm asking you nicely, please---see the forest for the trees
and don't ignore my wishes, calling all us women, bitches
when you see I'm breaking dishes constantly...

I can't clean up this mess off of the floor---
I won't let you depress me anymore---
I know we have a kid---but we have really hit the skids,
and you will respect my wishes, or I'll feed you to the
fishes
before I let you try to use your hugs and kisses, anymore

I will stand up to you, so help me, Lord---
You're not the man I married, I'm so bored---
This baby that I carried deserves a family that's not
harried
and a childhood stored up with God knows, so much
more---

"Fools Suffer Gladly"
by Andrea J. Kramer on Bastille Day,
July 14, 2006

I can't love you anymore from day to day
You keep on stoppin' me at the door,
to say you'll change
I have always tried to see your point,
and not end things with a fight
But you play mind games all the time,
and think you're always right…So I just say---

Baby, don't hold on, when it's no good---
You say your words are just misunderstood---
But you block me from the door
when I can't take it anymore,
and say that I'm the one who causes you to pour
another, to remain.

So Baby, take a big step back, and let me go---
Stop with all the lies---and don't put on a show---
I've got my ducks all in a row, and I'm not some domino
to fall face first in a long line---of desperate women who
won't say "No".

Fools suffer gladly, without say---day to day
I'm not your damn housekeeper without pay---
hey, hey, hey

81

Oh Baby, don't hold on when it's no longer good---
You say your words are just misunderstood---

But I can't clean up this mess,
and I won't let myself get all depressed,
or let you use your hugs and kisses---
no regrets---just let me go---

"It's Sometime In The Morning"
by Bradley A. Johnson &
Andrea J. Kramer on August 10, 2006

It's one o'clock in the morning,
and I'm lying in my bed---
"So many things went wrong",
are the thoughts inside my head.
Were we not the "right" in life,
when all the rest went wrong?
Maybe I'll give in on this, and call and play it strong ...
(or: "Maybe I'll give up on this, and call, and play
along"...)

I have tried
Man, I have cried
Because you're not around
I lost my pride, when you left my side...
and the world's not crashing down.

Now it's two o'clock in the mornin'---
and I'm trying to fall asleep---
(Tossing) Twisting and turning from side to side,
wondering who you'll meet...
I rise up again and see the clock,
and now it's four a.m.---
Like a broken key inside a lock---
I'm stuck on you and them

But, I have tried and
Man, I have cried
Because you're not around---
I have pride when you're at my side
and the world's not crashing down.
(or: I lost my pride, when you left my side...
and the world came crashing down.)

More time goes by and I have to start
getting ready for my day---
But the realization that we're apart---
just gets in the way...

I have tried and, Man,
I have cried
because you're not around---
I have pride when you're at my side---
and the world's not crashing down---
(or: I lost my pride, when you left my side...
and the world came crashing down.)

"There's Something Really Wrong"
by Andrea J. Kramer on September 6, 2006

There's something really wrong with men
who (me when I) say one thing and do another
There's nothing at all strong with them (me/us)
when they (I/we) act like it's no bother

But I can tell you that I've never been my brother's keeper
I get so paranoid sometimes... I imagine the Grim Reaper
Better to get a dog when their care is similar but cheaper

I lie awake at night counting all the ones
I knew before him (her)
I need a break some times when I blame
all who did precede him (her)

It all adds up to this,
that my world could be a whole lot deeper
I went and settled for a man (someone)
who's simply not a pleaser

So look at me and say that there'll be hell to pay
if you don't try to reach her
And listen to your woman
when she stands there like a preacher

Like a maiden in distress
Like a woman in duress

Like a child who needs care
Tell her you'll always be there

Like a baby who needs water
Like a model son or daughter

Like a bride going to the altar
Tell her you will never falter

And then she will count her blessings,
confessing she still loves you too---
Angels dance above you singing---
There's still romance in whispering "I love you."

"I Love You So"
by Andrea J. Kramer on November 9, 2006

Look how far we've come

Memories and then some

Acknowledging our past

They said we'd never last---

But we showed them a thing or two---proving that I love
you, God, how much I love you,

yeah, I really love you---

Look how far we've been---
The blaming game's the real sin---It used to make my
head spin

I thought I always could win

True, we had some fights---real knockdown, drag-outs,
and sleepless nights---

but there's no up-hill climb, without us stumbling from
time to time

What matters here the most, is all that happiness you
bring---Filling my life with everything

That lovers feel is destiny---and wouldn't trade for
anything

I love you so---God knows how much you mean to me,
couldn't sleep without you next to me---couldn't dream
of being anything

I love you so---you are all my days and nights, I don't
care about those fights---
Who cares who's ever wrong or right---

I need you so---you give me strength to breathe---that's
why I'll never leave---I love you so

"Half-Way Break"
by Andrea J. Kramer
on December 28, 2006 (my birthday)

How'd I get there-----
Where'd I come from---
Took some money, seems so funny---
how'd I fit in
What's this income
Now I'm someone

How'd I get here---
someone else steer---
Before I crash and burn---
so much for me to learn
How'd I get there---
and how do I stay---

How'd I beat it
Did I meet it---
Or was I just sweet to it---

Here's the outcome
Now I'm someone---
just had to meet it---
head on to defeat it
and rise above the pain---
will my soul remain---

Half-way break is all it takes to be a man
No mistake, I appreciate all that I have---
and who I am---but how'd I get this way---
and will I always jam along while the musicians play---

Half-way break

"Half-Way Break"
by Andrea J. Kramer
on December 28, 2006 (my birthday)
(revised copy with chorus)

How'd I get here---
Where'd I come from---
Took some money, seems so funny---
how'd I fit in---
Here's the outcome---

Now I'm someone---
just had to meet it head on to defeat it
and rise above the pain---
while my soul remains---

Half-way break is all it takes to be a man
No mistake, I appreciate all that I have and who I am
But how'd I get this way and will I always jam along
while the musicians play my new release
and next hit song

What's this income---
Now I'm someone---
How'd I get here--- someone else steer---
Before I crash and burn--- will I ever learn---

How'd I beat it---
Did I meet it--- or was I just sweet to it---

Half-way break is all it takes to be a man---
No mistake, I appreciate all that I have and who I am
But how'd I get this way and always jam along
while the musicians play my new release and next big
song

2007

"My Little Oasis"
by Andrea J. Kramer on Easter Sunday, April 8, 2007

I grew up with the finer things
Designer dresses and name brand jeans
My father was a kidney doctor
My mother was a silly shopper
They raised me, to be spoiled rotten
sooner or later, I had forgotten

money and appearance were not
what makes me real
Rolling hills and wide open spaces,
was what I needed to feel

So I bought the farm and all its land
My little Oasis in the sand
Cows and horses, chicks and ducks
Didn't cost me a million bucks

Yes, I bought the farm and all its land
My little Oasis in the sand
Cows and horses, chicks and ducks
Didn't cost me a million bucks

It makes me feel just like a Queen
Never could get into that "Society" scene
My parents will never understand
that what makes me happy is miles of land.

Yes, I bought the farm and all its land
My little Oasis in the sand
Cows and horses, chicks and ducks,
and it didn't cost me a million bucks!

"I Never Believed Me"
by Andrea J. Kramer on Bastille Day, July 14, 2007

I never believed me---wo---wo
I let him deceive me---oh yeah.
He finally freed me---wo---wo
When he broke my heart.

We had something special---wo---wo
No walking on egg shells---oh no.
We said what we wanted---wo---wo
He kept me in stitches---and played his part.

I never expected---to be brought to my knees.
Her name is Rebecca---and she did as she pleased.
A reckoning's coming---her day of truth.
She'll go back where she came from---some place in
Duluth.

I never believed me---wo---wo
I let him deceive me---oh yeah.
He finally freed me---wo---wo
When my heart felt broke.

Now, it's no joking matter---no---no
When he told me he'd had her, in our house.
Well, I'm laughing and crying---oh yeah
'Cause I'm nobody's mouse---oh no.

He said, "Honey, wait a minute---do I have to move
out??"
I called up a locksmith---changed the locks in the house.
He cried on the doorstep, I was a voyeur---
He knew what was coming, a divorce lawyer.

I never believed me---wo---wo
I let him deceive me---oh yeah.
He finally freed me---wo---wo
When my heart felt broke.

"That's A Tall Order"
by Andrea J. Kramer on July 22 & 26, 2007

I looked at my babies playing in the dirt, hoping each
day, they'd never get hurt.
But a mother's job is to worry and weep---pray they're
safe, and not lose sleep.
Kiss their tears and dry their faces.
Ease their fears and tie their laces.
Reappear each morning to wake them---
be sincere when the bus driver takes them.

Later that day, hear the brakes at the corner---
cookies in hand, and a cool pitcher of water.
Understand, they won't be little forever---
soon a young man and a beautiful daughter.

All I can, and all I am is wrapped up
in making them a fine woman and man.
That's a tall order, such a tall order, that's a tall order.

Know that women all over the world go through this.
Even across the border, they seal it with a kiss.
No fretting and no regretting, just heading forward.
That's a tall order, what a tall order, that's a tall order---
That's a tall order, such a tall order, that's a tall order.

All I can, and all I am is wrapped up
in making them a fine woman and man.
That's a tall order, what a tall order, that's a tall order.
That's a tall order, such a tall order, that's a tall order.

"He's Got Me Jealous"
by Andrea J. Kramer on August 1, 2007

Well, here he is, he's in my life,
like a seeing eye dog, he knows he's right.
Being apart, for us, is hard to do,
it drives a wedge, all the way through.
I struggle with it when he makes me mad.
I juggle the kids and love their Dad.
But you know there are times when I just want my way.
No ands, ifs or buts, just a pleasant day.

Oh, I struggle with his wilily ways
His goof-ball habits and his know-it-all gaze
His rugged looks when they make a pretty girl stare
He's got me jealous, and doesn't care

Well, what can I say, I am his wife,
it's part of the package, he's my shining knight.
My four leaf clover, my lucky charm,
if it were over, I'd of heard an alarm.
I've got to relax, and just take in some air,
these are the facts, does he even care?
Of course he does, I'm just splitting hairs---
it's that way of his---it's so unfair.

Oh, I struggle with his wilily ways
His goof-ball habits and his know it all gaze
His rugged looks when they make a pretty girl stare
He's got me jealous, and doesn't care

"Does She Listen And Go"
by Andrea J. Kramer on August 2, 2007

Here she comes again, back into my life---
like a homing pigeon, she knows the flight.
She assumes she's welcome anytime,
but her crazy moods, can change on a dime.
I've said it once, I've said it before,
if you're planning on leaving,
then stay away from my door.

Does she listen and go---hell no, hell no
If she is here to stay---I'll get out of her way

To me it seems just down right nuts,
she sharpens that edge of hers like a knife that cuts.
I sort of dread it when she starts out all nice,
because her way is to laugh, then begin to slice.
But what can I do when I love her to death?
Will she ever change? I won't hold my breath.

Does she listen and go---hell no, hell no
If she is here to stay---I'll get out of her way

Man, what would my family say---
she's got a pride about her, and an attitude.
I can hear my Mama start to pray---
Lord, she'd say, Don't let her start a family feud.
I see the Preacher, bow his head and pray aloud---
Son, you're stuck with her so don't be proud.

Does she listen and go---hell no, hell no
If she is here to stay---I'll get out of her way
Does she listen and go---hell no, hell no
If she is here to stay---I'll get out of her way

"Angels On Earth"
by Andrea J. Kramer on August 24, 2007

Long time coming, angels on earth,
brothers and sisters, we know their worth.
But if we persist in denying their point,
the waters of Jesus will barely anoint.

I've lived long enough to know a sign when I see it.
I've sinned long enough to know
that "good" means to be it.
So all that I ask is for God to keep sending us
angels on earth, more angels on earth.
Like the second coming, a major rebirth
of angels on earth, more angels on earth.

Brothers and sisters let me tell you a tale,
God does let angels set us a sail.
Like Jonah in the ocean, swallowed up by that whale,
God will protect us because we are frail.

Long time coming, this feeling of hope,
brothers and sisters, we barely can cope.
But if we resign ourselves to a much bigger plan,
then we can remind ourselves of the purpose of man.

God, please keep sending us angels on earth,
for the greater good and for mans' rebirth.
God, please keep sending us angels on earth,
for the greater good and for mans' rebirth.

"All That"
by Andrea J. Kramer on August 26, 2007

Look at my babies, what pretty young ladies
they've turned out to be.
Maybe it's crazy but I'm feeling dazed at
how time reaches out for me.

I turn around and the years have gone by,
feet on the ground, I'm as level as the
Rock of Gibraltar.
But so much has happened since I stood with
my man at the altar.

Seasons change and family remains,
it's the good in us---oh, all that good in us.
So much good in us that God intends to share,
so much good in us, it's all my heart can bear.

He and I both put food on the table,
like a golden rope we are strong and we are stable.
I cook for them from the Alpha to the Omega,
he grins and says, "Honey, can you pass the potatoes"?

I look after them, and he returns the favor,
it's the values we credit to our girls' behavior.
Better to pass the time like a beautiful wind chime,
letting us know when the cool breezes blow.

Seasons change and family remains,
it's the good in us---oh, all that good in us.
So much good in us that God intends to share,
so much good in us, it's all my heart can bear.

Seasons change and family remains,
it's the good in us---oh, all that good in us.
So much good in us that God intends to share,
so much good in us, it's all my heart can bear.

"Survivor At Large"
by Andrea J. Kramer on August 28, 2007

Well, I'd be a liar if I didn't get tired from time to time.
My mother inspired me to get hired, but not part-time.
I work at staying the way I am, you work at being free.
I sure hope that it's worth our family,

'Cause I've taken over.
I am a survivor and I've taken over.
I won't be fired, I'm still in charge.
I've taken over, survivor at large.

I get up each morning, and start the day.
Put everybody first, isn't that just the way.
Drop off the kids at school, then pull up to work.
Put in a forty-hour week, and wait for the perks.

Yes, I've taken over.
I am a survivor and I've taken over.
I won't be fired, I'm still in charge.
I've taken over, survivor at large.

I come home each night to a life full of lies.
You soon follow, what a sight for sore eyes.
I know it can be better, if we'd just communicate.
But my patience has run out, and I will no longer wait.

So, I've taken over, I am still in charge.
Yeah, I've taken over, survivor at large.

107

"Tell Me I Don't Know You"
by Andrea J. Kramer on August 29 & 30, 2007

What makes up a country life---
some good memories when it all went right.
Others that leave a lump in my throat,
or get my goat when I'm up late at night.

Trying to plan the next day in my head,
sooner or later, you'll be coming to bed.
I can wait until I hear your footsteps in the hall,
liquor on your breath, you're still eleven feet tall.

Tell me I don't know you, when we are a team
Hell, I can only show you what you mean to me
Tell me I don't know you, when we are meant to be
Sell me stock in the Brooklyn Bridge, if you think
you don't know me

You're fast asleep, I'm still making my list.
If you were a Mr. Mom, that'd be quite a twist.
I love being a country girl, and a good man's wife,
but lately you seem restless, and not quite right.

Tell me I don't know you, when we are a team
Hell, I can only show you what you mean to me
Tell me I don't know you, when we are meant to be
Sell me stock in the Brooklyn Bridge,
if you think you don't know me

Whatever's bothering you, we can work it through.
This country woman's life is so devoted to you.
Like our parents before us, and our grandparents, too,
You know me…and I sure know you.

Tell me I don't know you, when we are a team
Hell, I can only show you what you mean to me
Tell me I don't know you, when we are meant to be
Sell me stock in the Brooklyn Bridge, if you think
you don't know me---

"Always Stand Out"
by Andrea J. Kramer on September 2, 2007

All of my life, I wanted to be known,
but my mother exaggerated my talent,
or so I thought.

She encouraged me to get up on stage,
and play the guitar she bought.
I was nervous, and I felt tense,
but she swore to me, it'd be time well spent.

I got up there, and did my best.
Sang to my heart's content, and relied on the rest.
But, the funny thing is, that what it's all about,
is that people who don't fit in at first,
are the ones who always stand out.

Always stand out
Even though it's round-a-bout
Follow your heart
You just have to start

Now I'm grown, and out on that stage,
Truth be known, my mother's to blame.
But I'm glad she pushed me in front of that mike,
because singing for y'all is such a big part of my life.

Always stand out
Even though it's round-a-bout
Follow your heart, and
Make the waters part

Always stand out
Even though it's round-a-bout
Follow your heart
You just have to start

"It Takes A Long Time"
by Andrea J. Kramer on September 8 & 9, 2007,
inspired by Michael Ken

Earl Connelly and Keith Whitley
used to keep me up late at night.
I listened to them on the radio
after kissing my parents good night.
I turned the sound down low,
so they thought I went to sleep.
But my hopes of being in a show,
were what lingered in my dreams.

Well nearly twenty years went by
when one of my dreams came true.
I wound up playing my guitar one night
as a singer/song writer too.
I was up at the Eden Fair Grounds,
playing with my band,
when out of the blue came walking,
a tall, slender man.

He said his name was Earl T. Connelly,
but I already knew who he was.
I saw the image of Keith Whitley by his side
coming off of that bus.
He motioned me to come over,
for what turned out to be a pretty long chat,
and said some words I still think over,
on stage in my cowboy hat.

He said Son, it takes a long time,
from where you are to this place I'm at
But I know you're gonna get there,
it's just a matter of fact
Yes, it takes a real long time,
from where you are to this place I'm at
But I know you're gonna get there,
it's just a matter of fact

Man, Earl Connelly came down off of his bus that night,
to tell me and my band that we sounded---alright.
With a twinkle in his eye in the pale moonlight,
he took a stand, that the future would be bright.

He said, Son, it takes a long time,
from where you are to this place I'm at
But I know you're gonna get there,
it's just a matter of fact
Yes, it takes a real long time,
from where you are to this place I'm at
But I know you're gonna get there,
it's just a matter of fact

"Long Legs And Country Songs"
by Andrea J. Kramer on September 9, 2007

While out at my favorite watering hole,
I sat there bored, lookin' for the beautiful and the bold.
When in walks this pretty young thing,
with a set of long legs leading up to a g-string.
I said, Damn, pretty lady where you been all my life, but I
said it under my breath, with no chance in sight.
To my amazement she came on over, her hair and eyes
full of moonlight, and asked me out right, what exactly I
liked.

I like long, lean legs and country songs
I like tight blue jeans covering up those thongs
I like women in red and blankets off the bed
I like a brain and spunk and country fun

Well, Cowboy, she said, don't be messin' with my head,
'cause it just turns out, I can meet your dreams
and let it all hang out.
Damn, I thought, can this be real, pour me another drink,
and I'll show her how I feel.
I like long, lean legs and country songs
I like tight blue jeans covering up those thongs
I like women in red and blankets off the bed
I like a brain and spunk and country fun

"Long Legs And Country Songs"
by Andrea J. Kramer on September 9, 2007,
revised on September 11, 2007

While out at my favorite watering hole,
I sat there bored, lookin' for the beautiful and the bold.
Then in walks this pretty young thing,
with a set of long legs leading up to a g-string.

I said, Damn, pretty lady where you been all my life,
 but I said it under my breath, with no chance in sight.
To my amazement she came on over,
her hair and eyes full of moonlight,
and asked me out right, what exactly, I liked.

I like long, lean legs and country songs
I like tight blue jeans showin' off a those thongs
I like a woman in red, and blankets off the bed
I like a brain and spunk, and to get 'um drunk!

Well Cowboy, she said, don't be messin' with my head,
'cause it just turns out, I can meet your dreams,
and let it all hang out.
Damn, I thought, can this be real,
pour me another drink, and I'll show her how I feel.

I like long, lean legs and country songs
I like tight blue jeans showin' off a those thongs
I like a woman in red, and blankets off the bed
I like a brain and spunk, and to get um drunk!

115

"If I Looked As Good As You Do"
by Andrea J. Kramer on September 13, 2007
(Third stanza added on Rosh Hashanah)

There are people who are angels,
then there are people who are not.
Some are looking out for number one,
when put on the spot.
Everybody's got a gift to share,
whether it's good or not...
Some even have those gifts to spare,
depending on what they've got.

If I looked as good as you do,
then I'd share yourself with me
If I stood up straight and tall,
then I'm no case for charity
If I put up with it all,
would you share yourself with me?
Well the writing's on the wall,
you and me got chemistry

There are children who are smaller,
but their spirits aren't weak.
There are elders at the town hall,
who will turn the other cheek.
All of us fall in between them,
some are smart, and others' pretty.
Whether hiding wings or different motives,
we're just trying to make a living.

116

If I looked as good as you do,
then I'd share yourself with me
If I stood up straight and tall,
then I'm no case for charity
If I put up with it all,
would you share yourself with me?
'Cause the writing's on the wall, babe,
you and me got chemistry

From the country to the city,
people see what they believe.
No matter what they tell us,
we all have that one same need.
Everybody's got a point to make,
and hope that they look good.
When it's live and there no out-takes,
people do just as they should.

If I looked as good as you do,
then I'd share yourself with me
If I stood up straight and tall,
then I'm no case for charity

If I put up with it all,
would you share yourself with me?
'Cause the writing's on the wall, babe,
you and me got chemistry

"Life Is For Leavin'"
by Andrea J. Kramer on November 24, 2007
inspired by Michael Ken

There are three things in life we do,
 and this is number one
We grow up and leave our parents,
when they say we've had our fun
We move on in life and us guys get our wives,
and start our families
But if we think twice about what's right---
we may not always keep our family tree

Life is for leavin'
Now, none of that grievin'
Some of us knew we weren't always right
Time for change means throwin' in the towel,
not stayin' in the fight

Leavin' a marriage is the second thing,
we sometimes have to do
Doesn't mean we don't still love you,
just because we're through
The final thing is leavin' this life,
with a fond memory or two
But don't you think we didn't try our best,
to be Mr. Right for you!

Life is for leavin'
Now, none of that grievin'
Some of us knew we weren't always right
Time for change means throwin' in the towel,
not stayin' in the fight

Life is for leavin'
Now, none of that grievin'
Some of us knew we weren't always right
Time for change means throwin' in the towel,
not stayin' in the fight

"Baby, The Road To Home"
by Andrea J. Kramer on November 24, 2007

Baby, the road to home is so far, far away
I'm writing you this letter with so much to say
Our plans for a future together were interrupted,
good
The doctors say my sutures will hold me together...
should
But whatever the outcome---whether I can walk or not
This letter is in no way, to put you on the spot

If you don't want to wait for me---it's o.k. to say "no"
If you don't want to stay with me---I'll have to let you go
If you don't want to wait for me---it's o.k. to say "no"
If you don't want to stay with me... then just say so

Pity doesn't keep a man and woman
in each other's arms for long
Sympathy is one thing,
but courage and compassion are for the strong
Whether I lose my legs or not,
is not what makes me whole
Being a man without them is one thing,
but you not wanting me is what will take its toll

If you don't want to wait for me---it's o.k. to say "no"
If you don't want to stay with me---I'll have to let you go
If you don't want to wait for me---it's o.k. to say "no"
If you don't want to stay with me... then just say so

If you don't want to wait for me---it's o.k. to say "no"
If you don't want to stay with me---I'll have to let you go
If you don't want to wait for me---it's o.k. to say "no"
If you don't want to stay with me... then just say so

"Country Music And Long Sexy Legs"
by Andrea J. Kramer on November 25, 2007
inspired by Michael Ken

Every Saturday night, I go out to the Rhinestone Grill
Got no intention of leavin' until I've had my fill
The music's loud and the women are hot
The natives are restless, and we'll start to rock

Country music and long sexy legs
get my attention with an affectionate gaze
Baby, I want you, do you want me too??
If the answer's yes, let's have a dance or two

The music's still goin', we're feelin' real good
This woman comes towards me, as if she should
Then we'll sit and have a couple of beers---
I'll find something to say so confidence appears

We'll get up to leave as I say
"Let's get out of here"
She takes my car keys at the pick-up, and says
"Which way do I steer"?

Oh, baby, Country music and long sexy legs
get my attention with an affectionate gaze
Baby, I want you, do you want me too??
If the answer is "yes", let's have a dance or two

Yeah, we'll get up to leave as I say
"Let's get out of here"
She takes my car keys at the pick-up, and says
"Which way do I steer"?

Charlie Helmick's 2005
"Farmer In The Fast Lane"
revised by Andrea J. Kramer on November 28, 2007

I get home for the night and watch the evening news
I think to myself what would Bo Cephus do??
My "family tradition" was to watch the tube and drink
Goin' twenty miles an hour in my brain---
I've got time to think!

I agree (say) a Country boy knows how to survive
My hours of work are not just nine to five
Seven days a week I go slow and steady
Twenty miles an hour until I am ready

I'm a farmer in the fast lane
Draggin' my trailer chains
Still nursin' my John Deere wound...
Waitin' on the world to go BOOM!

Haulin' my crops from town to town
Bouncin' and shakin' all the way, down
Twenty miles an hour---still got the power
To be a farmer in the fast, fast lane!
Got the traffic backed up for nearly three city blocks
Like to shoot the breeze with folks, and take some stock
In the fact that whether I'm haulin' ass or not---
my tractor-trailer is all I got!!

I'm a farmer in the fast lane
With a bank note and a mortgage to pay
Draggin' my trailer chains from spot to spot
Got more plantin' to do...
Waitin' on the world to go BOOM!

"Lexington Road"
by Andrea J. Kramer on December 13-16, 2007

Lexington Road is where I hold my memories dear
As they unfold, I know my sweet heart is near
Sooner or later... here or there
It'll all come together, with hardly a care

Lexington Road is where I have found golden hair
As I was told, there's a beautiful woman there
Although the trail's cold, I still feel heat from you
Beautiful and bold, you need me to come through for you

I left you there, and went on my merry way
With not so much as a care, I went astray that day
But here I am now, back from the dead it seems
If you can believe me, you never left my dreams

Lexington road is where I have found golden hair
As I was told, there's a beautiful woman there
Although the trail's cold, I still feel heat from you
Beautiful and bold, you need me to come through for you

Give me a chance to prove that I have finally changed
If your father were here, a shotgun be arranged
Let me convince you now, that I'm a sure bet
Let me move back with you,
and I promise you no regrets

Lexington Road is where
I have found golden hair
As I was told,
there's a beautiful woman there
Although the trail's cold,
I still feel heat from you
Beautiful and bold,
you need me to come through for you

2008

"When A Woman Loves"
by Andrea J. Kramer on January 2, 2008,
idea inspired by Dave Statzer

When I look back on all I've tried...
and all I've done was not a lie
I understand what it means to feel...
that caring deep is always real

But, the thing that sticks with me the most...
with what I've seen from coast to coast
Is that when a woman loves,
she loves with all her heart,
and that's not true of a man

And the reason it's not true of a man is because...
a man loves with what ever he can

He can love with many things
like diamond rings,
and a house with a picket fence
He can love with many things,
like flowers in the spring,
and a Bentley or a pick-up---
whatever makes sense

He can love with casual sex
and gentle pecks on her cheek,
coming home from a date

He can love with the words "God bless"
or a nice long rest with her
in his arms when it's late

But what he just can't do is follow through
or wear his heart on his sleeve
Because what a man thinks,
is that he needs to piece, a plan together to leave

A woman stays and waits out the days,
and loves with all of her heart and soul
A man just needs to stay loose and free,
and say "marry me"... when he feels so bold
(or: when he's not too old)

He can love with many things like diamond rings,
and a house with a picket fence
He can love with many things,
like flowers in the spring,
and a Bentley or a pick-up---
whatever makes sense (or: whatever comes next)

He can love with casual sex
and gentle pecks on her cheek,
coming home from a date
He can love with the words "God bless"
or a nice long rest with her
in his arms when it's late

"Precious Time Of Day"
by Andrea J. Kramer on January 23, 2008

Why won't you ever give me back
that precious time of day...
when all I do is apologize,
and waste the day away
Thinking of you from the time I wake up ...
from moment to endless moment...
Drinking you in with my hot coffee in the morning,
and thinking you've been offering up your good name
to not seem boring

Changing our only chance to be happy in this life,
and maybe even ever lasting
When I try to see ahead, I am slowly dying
without you... as if forever fasting

Why won't you
Oh, why won't you
Give me back that time of day
When we were both together
and loneliness was a million miles away

Why won't you
Oh, why won't you
Give me back that time of day
When we were both together,
and loneliness was a million miles away

People say you can't save the world...
but I'll be damned, if I can't save this girl
My grandpa always told me to never loan three things,
your huntin' dog, shotgun or your pick-up
But he never mentioned anything about grandma...
which is probably why I'm so mixed up

So why won't you...
Yes, I say why won't you...
Oh, Darling why just won't ya...
give me back that time of day...

"Precious Day"
by Andrea J. Kramer
on January 23, & February 7, 2008

Why won't you ever give me back
that precious time of day...
when all I do is apologize,
and waste the day away
Thinking of you from the time I wake up...
from moment to endless moment...
Drinking you in with my hot coffee
in the morning,
and thinking you've been offering up your good name...
to not seem boring...
Telling me you'd stay right here...
spelling out to me to not stay clear
Changing our only chance to be happy in this life,
and maybe even ever lasting
When I try to see ahead,
I am slowly dying without you...
as if forever fasting

Why won't you
Oh, why won't you
Give me back that precious time of day
When we were both together
and loneliness was a million miles away
Why won't you

Oh, why won't you
Give me back that special time of day
When we were both together,
and loneliness was a million miles away

People say you can't save the world...
but I'll be damned if I can't save you, girl...
My grandpa always told me...
to never lose three things...
your huntin' dog, shotgun, or your pick-up...
But he never mentioned anything...
about grandma bein' one of those things...
which is probably why,
when it comes to you and me...
I'm so... damned... mixed up...

So... why... won't... you...
Yes, I say... why... won't... you...
Oh, Darling... just why won't ya...
give me back that... time of day...
that precious... time of day...
when we were both together...
and loneliness... was a million miles... away.

"I Saw Billy Joel on Oprah"
by Andrea J. Kramer on March 28, 2008

I saw Billy Joel on Oprah
with his twenty-three year old wife
She did all the talking,
while he reflected on his life
Oprah brought up his music,
but his wife just wanted to speak
She said her cooking was all he cared about,
and what there was to drink

I sat there for a moment
with my mouth gaped open a bit
Here was Billy Joel, an icon
and my idol, turning on a spit
He seemed tranquilized and mellow
to the point of no return
I watched Oprah shine a light on him,
and wait for the that long, slow burn

Come out Virginia and wake me from this dream
Tell me it ain't so, and that Billy Joel's redeemed
He had a drinking problem, this we know is true
But marrying a girl his daughter's age,
would get him on the news

I waited for him to agree with Oprah,
that he was still a legend
At least he got up off his seat,
 and sang a song without hesitation

But after the commercial break,
when he got back into his chair
He answered questions like some old guy,
and just sat back and stared

Come out Virginia and wake me from this dream
Tell me it ain't so, and that Billy Joel's still mean
Come out Virginia and give me that famous sign
Tell me it ain't so, and that Billy Joel's just fine

"She Don't Know What Love's About"
by Andrea J. Kramer on July 22, 2008

I thought I couldn't write any more
My mind was as empty as a sold-out store
I tossed and turned over what she (he) said
When my feet hit the floor from my un-made bed
I rose to face another painful day
Her (his) career was all she (he) needed anyway
So why do I still carry a torch
When it's obvious we're gonna end in divorce
(or: we're gonna get a divorce)

She don't know what love's about
She'll take the stage with a big shout-out
She threw me back like some small trout
'Cause she don't know what love's about

We made a life or so I thought
From all the many things we bought
A house, a Catty, a big ol' truck
Private schools, for thousands of bucks
The kids were growing up just fine
Occasionally, she'd want more and whine
But I just wrote it off to spoiled talk
I never thought she'd actually walk

'Cause she don't know what love's about
She'll take the stage with a big shout-out
She threw me back like some small trout
and she don't know what love's..... About.

"Mahogany, Mine"
by Andrea J. Kramer on September 22, 2008

She's as delicate, and just as light as pine---
She's as earthy as a homemade bottle of wine
Who's as rich in flavor as grapes growin' on the vine?
My mahogany woman, my beautiful woman---
I can't believe she's mine

Mine oh mine, my amazing Mahogany, she's mine
Finer than fine, aren't words good enough to describe
Mine oh mine, my amazing Mahogany, she's mine
Did I die and go to Heaven for this angel who is mine

In my time, there have been many but not as fine as her...
In my line of work there have been plenty
but none with her sweet curves
When I look back on when I'm twenty
and the world was at my feet
I had no idea at this age,
she'd be the one I needed to meet ...

Mine oh mine, my amazing Mahogany, she's mine
Finer than fine, aren't words good enough to describe
Mine oh mine, my amazing Mahogany, she's mine
Did I die and go to Heaven for this angel to be mine

"Born With Everything, Wanting Nothing"
by Andrea J. Kramer on September 24, 2008

Hearing fateful voices...
the night I became alive
Second sight, that very night,
caused my Mom to survive
An angel came and whispered
that her due date would be late
Daddy lit his pipe to smoke,
for what would seem, a pretty long wait

Born with everything, wanting nothing
But to feel loved and safe
Voices from above would agree
All I needed to be was... free

Both parents being controlling...
didn't know this wasn't love
"Emotional roller-coaster,"
is the term I'm thinking of
But for a couple miscalculations,
I might not have turned out right
I stand here today before you,
but for the grace of God and His great light

Born with everything, wanting nothing
But to feel loved and safe
Voices from above would agree
All I needed to be was... free

When I think of my survival...
and what I wanted, to feel whole
It's nature versus nurture...
like a mare with her new foal

Be whoever you are being,
as long as that's your very best
Everyone's a star in their own way
and so, they're rightly blessed

Born with everything, wanting nothing
But to feel loved and safe
Voices from above would agree
All I needed to be was... free

"Everybody Gets"
by Andrea J. Kramer on October 3 & 4, 2008

Everybody gets what they deserve in life.
Everybody regrets it when they weren't right.
Everybody frets when they think they've missed their moment.
What they seem to forget is that they never really own it.

There are moments that come once or twice in a lifetime...
Like OJ finally going away for A lonnnng time.
What if I'm your moment... and you are also mine?
Not a life sentence, that I would ever mind!

Everybody gets what they deserve
Whether they drive straight or take a swerve
Life is gonna throw ya' some serious curves
Yeah, everybody gets what they deserve

What if we were guilty of love at first sight
Didn't seem to bother you that very first night
I don't want to turn this into another fight
I say son, let's get it done and finally do what's right

Everybody gets what they deserve
Whether they drive straight or take a swerve
Life is gonna throw ya' some serious curves
Yeah, everybody gets..... what they deserve

"This Is The One"
by Andrea J. Kramer on October 9, 2008

This is the one, I've been waiting for
No more trying to be different, anymore
Originality is my middle name...
Not copying other's in their reach for fame...

Tired of holding on to the dream
Tired of thinking up any more schemes
Willing to let go of the glamorous past
Willing to say no...to making it last

Ahhh, ahhh, ahhhh, ahh, ahh, ahh...
I'm in my own league when it comes to that
I've managed to keep what is mine this long
I was able to leave, and live out this song

Some will come and some will go...
Making The One is all I know...
Coming up with a song to make you see
That all you need...is to believe in me

Ahhh, ahhh, ahhhh, ahh, ahh, ahh...
I'm in my own league when it comes to that
I've managed to keep what is mine this long
I was able to leave, and live out this song

No need to reinvent the wheel...
if you don't like it, it's no big deal (it's got no appeal)
Stop changing my words inside your head—
admit I'm right, (better) and put it to bed

Ahhh, ahhh, ahhhh, ahh, ahh, ahh...
I'm in my own league when it comes to that
I've managed to keep what is mine this long
I was able to leave, and live out this song,
and remain this strong

"Everybody Needs To Know"
or "Strong Points Are"
by Andrea J. Kramer
on October 8 and 18 and November 14, 2008

Everybody needs to know their limits,
and likewise what their strong points are...
Those they need to embrace and not erase,
when they are not always feeling up to par...

Skill, is not just a matter of will...
but a God given gift to us all
If you don't learn this in life...
oh, how the weak will inherit and oh yes...
how the mighty will fall

Russian Roulette is an obvious regret
if the bullet game is not won
When you bluff your life, there's one sure thing...
your winning streak will be done

So think it through and look how I do
at admitting my weaknesses and flaws
Knowing what our true strong points are...
give us all good reason for pause

There will come a day when we can say,
"I feel privileged to pray to God"
It will come our way to feel thankful and blessed...
for that all appreciative nod

Stay away from the pride that tares us apart,
and instead acknowledge our best
Then leave it up to your natural born gifts...
and the world should do the rest...

"All I Need Is KKL"
by Andrea J. Kramer, revised on November 16, 2008

You think I'm kidding? well, I'm not kidding anymore...
So help me, I will walk you through this hallway to the
door...
'cause I don't need to hear this double talk anymore...
You know what it is, I need from you, and so does the
Lord, above... it's just so easy,
it's your kindness, kisses, love...

Yeah, I won't pine for you...or for your kindness, kisses,
love...
'cause I'm finished with those promised wishes
and all those endless hugs and kisses, yeah
I'd rather do the dishes than crave your
kindness, kisses, love.
No, I won't pine for you or ignore the fact...
you lack kindness, kisses, and... love...

2009

"Thank You For Everything"
by Andrea J. Kramer on February 13, 2009

I know I'm young...
have my whole life to live...
It's all been fun...
with more to take than give...
But, now I see...
that there's a place for me
An actual space for me...
to leave my own imprint

I can't believe this is happening
I'm crying and laughing
I'm singing my heart out
I'm learning what life's about

My luck is changing... I'm still remaining...
to sing a song for you...You made my dreams come true
So this is living... and finally giving back...
I've grown a lot this year... here are my smiles and tears...

I can't believe this is happening
I'm crying and laughing
I'm singing my heart out
I'm learning what life's about

Thank you for helping me...thank you for everything
Thank you for listening...and taking in everything
Thank you for being there...thank you for all your care
Thank you for liking me...thank you for fighting for me...

Thank you, American Idol...

"I'm Not The Perfect Person"
by Andrea J. Kramer on February 12, 2006,
revised August 15, 2006 and July 20, 2009

Well, it's been a while since you left that way---
 I play it over in my mind down to the very last day---
The only reason I could find,
that would make you take your things---
was that I didn't tell you, Darlin',
what tenderness you bring.

I thought my actions were enough---
that all you needed was my love---
But I was wrong not to say it (tell you) now and then, that
it's you I'm thinking of

Your picture's on my night stand
and I'm missing you in my heart---
I'm lovin' you with my eyes---
how did we get so far apart?

One shirt's left in my closet with your scent still part of it
(or: with your perfume still on it)
I can't bring myself to wash the thing, or just get rid of it
Because, I think of you before I sleep and then begin to
dream---
I never meant to disappoint or make you think I'm mean.

I just assumed you understood,
I'd drop the other shoe (I didn't have a clue)---
and maybe that I'm not the perfect person
you once knew.

Your picture's on my nightstand
and I'm missing you in my mind---
I'm lovin' you in my heart---
 someone like you's so (is so) hard to find.
I just assumed you understood,
I'd drop the other shoe (I didn't have a clue)---
and maybe that I'm not the perfect person
you once knew.

"Tank"
by Andrea J. Kramer on July 21, 2009,
revised from "Our Human Race"
written on July 18, 2007

Take me on home, brother...
the world's caving in
Take me on home, sister...
my head's starting to spin.
Don't leave me alone out here...
 I fought as hard as I could.
My kids aren't grown, so steer...
this train's (Tank's) headed for my neighborhood.

We still have a shot at life
before Jesus calls out our names---
If Heaven gets in the way,
we have only our selves to blame.
It may be a bumpy road,
but I'll use what might I have.
So pull me along this train, (Tank)
down that most righteous of paths.

My doorstep is where I'm at,
not in front of the Pearly Gates.
I thought we'd be laid out flat,
our leader claiming "what a waste".
But my brothers and sisters both,
said a saving grace, and did what they needed most,
protected our human race.

"Beautiful Days"
(on leave from Iraq)
by Andrea J. Kramer on May 13, 2005,
revised on July 25 & 28, 2009

Mama was bakin' a cherry pie,
and I looked up at the bright, blue sky
and thought baby, what a beautiful day

Dad was cuttin' the lawn in the (out) back,
and I realized I still had to pack
and thought baby, I have to go away

If only I didn't have to leave so soon,
but I have to be on a bus by noon
and catch a U.S. plane to hot desert terrain

I may not see you again this year, but
Darlin' I ask you to have no fear
Because I love you so just say---
What a beautiful day it is when you are here

Now look ahead and not backward,
although I'll be on tactical alert
across the desert plain---
don't make me have to explain

Mama will be reading a new cookbook,
and Daddy will be telling you to take a good look
and see---I'm defending our country

(or: Mama will be scrubbin' the pots and pans
when Daddy (or: Dad) comes in to wash his hands
or: Daddy comes in from tending the land
(or: Daddy finished lookin' at our land)…
and sees how sad we can be

Then Mama starts crying a tear or two
(or: Mama dries off a tear or two)
but Daddy (or: Dad tells her that this is what I do)
(or: understands that or: knows that) this is what I do,
and it's time for me to go away to defend our country)
(or Mama dried off a tear or two
and Daddy whispers softly "I love you",
and I thought Baby, I have no words to say
(or else repeat: "I have to go away")
(or: Mama was bringin' in the mail…
the day started out like a fairy tale,
as I waited for my sweet prince to wake
Then Daddy brings in the paper to read and Mama does
whatever her family needs and I know this is not a
mistake or:
You and I sit down to eat…
every moment together is tender and sweet,
but I know, I have some place to be
Daddy brings in the paper to read,
he prays this war will end,
Godspeed and for me not to be
so far from home and family
or: Daddy is watching the news online,
he says a quiet prayer for me to be fine,

so far from him and family
or: Mama's reading a new cookbook
and Daddy comes in and takes a good look
at the love he sees in you and me
or: at the beauty of you and me)

So look ahead and not backward,
although I'll be on tactical alert,
because you know it's true---
I had these beautiful days to spend with you
(or: Baby, thank God I had these beautiful days
to spend with you---
that's what's always going to get me through,
so I need you just to pray---
and say, I'll see you again one beautiful day.

"Keep It Simple, Cupid"
by Andrea J. Kramer on July 29, 2009,
idea inspired by A. Bard

What I love about you is, you're romantic
You get under my skin, it's like, pandemic
Then you go and change the rules on me
You think you're getting sympathy

But what I feel is that you're phony, not real
Could you possibly be more stupid??
Just keep it simple, Cupid
Just get it right, Cupid!

Don't delay, Cupid---
I'm at your mercy

"When Love Is Gone"
by Andrea J. Kramer on June 23, 2005,
revised on July 31, 2009

When love is gone
all is wrong
the birds (larks) forget to sing

When trust is strong
it won't be long
before love will fix (heal) all things

You can't imagine what I feel
When I believe (pretend) we aren't real
The images that cross my mind
are not some romance dime store find

The book of love that fills my heart
has paragraphs that set apart
the reasons why I need you so
and won't give up on... I don't know
(or: on you, or who, I know)

Some say that joy is in romance
(or: some say the fun is in the dance)
but I am stumbling in a trance
because your love for me is gone
and mine for you is still so strong

Don't let me down and go away
the sun won't shine and kids won't play---
darkness falls on (or over) those who pine
so when you're away, keep me in mind
(or: on your mind)

'Cause when you are gone
love's not in sight
I long for you each day and night
So hear this song (prayer) and understand
You are my heart, you are my man (woman)
(or:)
'Cause when you left me, and went out of sight
I longed for you each day and night
(or: every day and night)
So hear this song, and understand
You are my heart, my only (wo)man

2010

"Salacious Details"
by Andrea J. Kramer on August 5, 2005,
revised on March 11, 2010

What can I say
When you look away
My mind repeats how we would meet
One at a time we'd sneak outside
When we were asked, we simply lied

Salacious details are our own
No one should know until they're grown
How appetizing life can be---
It feeds that need inside of me

We'd find a way to be alone
Only the two of us condone
The acts between us were so nice
They would be bad---my only vice

Salacious details are our own
No one should know until they're grown
How appetizing lust can be
It feeds that hunger inside of me

After---we'd never have regrets
We'd joke and smoke a cigarette
What else could I possibly need---
return to work, pretend to read

Salacious details are our own
No one should know until they're grown
How satisfying lust can be
It feeds that need inside of me---

"Lovin' A Mysterious Man"
by Andrea J. Kramer
on December 23, 2005 / March 14, 2010

Well, here I am singin' my song---
When I collected my thoughts,
it took all day long,
just to say what is the God's honest truth.

I sat down on my favorite rocker,
on the front porch---
I can't believe, I held a torch
for this man livin' under my roof

What is worse, than a woman's curse,
of lovin' a mysterious man?
A good man who does bad things,
being charming whenever he can.

What's as hard as livin' large,
and not saving for a rainy day?
Thinkin' everything's o.k.,
while your kids go out to play.

What is worse than a woman's curse,
of lovin' a deceitful man?
A good man who does bad things,
being charming whenever he can.

All I can do, is hope I'm not at the end of my rope,
and I'll find the patience to forgive---
the stamina to find a job, the wherewithal to live.

Well, here I am singin' my song,
when I collected my thoughts, it took all day long,
just to say the way I feel.
I wish it weren't so damn real,
or there was some way I could appeal.

"I Need A Man"
Prologue by Andrea J. Kramer

I need a man, man, man, man, man, man, man
I need a guy, guy, guy-guy...guy...
I need a man, man, man, man, man---man
So, brother, let me try---

To find a man, man, man, man, man, man, man
To help me with my female pride...
I need a hand, hand, hand, hand, hand---man
To land a guy, guy, guy...

I need a man, man, man, man...man-man...man
I need a guy, guy, guy-guy, guy...
I need a man, man, man, man, man---man...
To not give up and Hide...

"Money Does"
by Andrea J. Kramer on August 2, 2005,
revised on March 15, 2010

I have played in the big man's league---
money, honey is my only creed.
So, Baby, maybe you will see and read---
money does really grow on trees,
money does really grow on trees.

Why be married to a fat, rich cat---
if I can't spend it, and be all that??
I want to be an Aristocrat,
shop and spend like a Hilton brat!!
So, Baby, maybe you will see and read---
money does really grow on trees!
You, don't have to drop down to your knees---
just look up and count the money leaves!

Money does really grow on trees,
money does focus all my needs...
If you think I am so shallow then,
come with me, and I'll let you spend...

There's an art to being a Sophisticate...
all it takes is a great big shopping list!
When you buy, you are so powerful...
Rodéo Drive, takes more than an hour full!
Harry Winston and my Tiffany---
I see them both as an epiphany!!

You don't have to drop down to your knees---
just look up and count the money leaves!

Money does really grow on trees,
money does focus all my needs.
Yes, money does really grow on trees,
money does really grow on trees!

"I Like Barbara Bush"
by Andrea J. Kramer on June 19, 2005,
revised on May 8, 2010

I like my Coke and Wild Turkey
I like my smokes and my beef jerky
Now you might think this sounds real quirky...
but I like Barbara Bush

I like the way she raised our President, married one and
wasn't hesitant... supported the Bush men... all the way
back when

She let her grandkids make public fun of her,
I like the way
she backs their father and mother,
and lets them do and say
what is the American way...

I like the way she doesn't let the Democrats---
turn her family into back-biting bureaucrats---
just keeps them pointed straight---
right towards a withdrawal from Kuwait!

I like my Coke and Wild Turkey
I like my smokes and my beef jerky
Normally, I like my women perky
but not Miss Barbara Bush!

"Bible Verses To Spare!"
by Andrea J. Kramer on September 10, 2007
revised on September 11, 2007
and August 25, 2010
inspired by Penny at Lowe's

I got a story to tell about a woman I met...
As soon as I get it off my chest,
I'll have no more regrets.
I thought she was a teacher
by the way she wore her hair...
But turned out she was a preacher,
with Bible verses to spare!

She told me not to take the Lord's name in vain
Or she wouldn't listen and she wouldn't remain
She said saying "Damn it" was a federal offense
And that she wouldn't date me unless I repent

Well, Hell I thought what a holy roller she was,
I only swore when I'm mad, just because.
If everybody was as Bible thumping as that,
they wouldn't have any words to say
that matched their acts!

Sometimes, it's good to let off a little steam,
the Lord don't care, it ain't that mean.
People cuss because they can...
if we forget to repent, we can't all be damned!!

I tried to explain this as best I could,
but she started to wail, that I misunderstood.
She said I best talk with God about my profanity,
and that only He would forgive me for my insanity.

She told me not to take the Lord's name in vain
Or she wouldn't listen and she'd only complain
She said saying "Damn it" was a federal offense
And that she wouldn't date me unless I repent

She told me not to take the Lord's name in vain
Or she wouldn't listen and she wouldn't remain
She said saying "Damn it" was a federal offense
And that she wouldn't date me unless I repent

"Prayer"
by Andrea J. Kramer in July of 2009,
idea inspired by A. Bard, revised in 2010

Good for the good and good from the bad...
good for the soul is never so sad
as when (or with) love and good health,
love takes its toll
but more good than bad,
is good for the soul.

Made in the USA
Charleston, SC
16 March 2012